Awesome Bugs

BUTTERFLIES

 and MOTHS

Anna Claybourne

FRANKLIN WATTS
London · Sydney

© Aladdin Books Ltd 2004

Produced by:
Aladdin Books Ltd
28 Percy Street
London W1T 2BZ

ISBN 0–7496–5490–2

First published in
Great Britain in 2004 by:
Franklin Watts
96 Leonard Street
London
EC2A 4XD

Editor:
Harriet Brown

Designer:
Flick, Book Design & Graphics

Illustrators:
Tony Swift, Philip Weare,
Norman Weaver
Cartoons: Jo Moore

Certain illustrations have
appeared in earlier books
created by Aladdin Books.

Printed in UAE

Contents

Introduction

In this book you can find out all about butterflies and moths. These amazing insects, with their delicately patterned wings, are probably the most beautiful and best-loved of all creepy crawlies. Inside these pages, you'll find out how butterflies and moths fly, what they eat, where they live, and how they grow up. You'll also discover amazing facts such as how butterflies taste with their feet, why moths fly into flames, how far some butterflies travel on their migration routes and much more!

Spot and count, and more fun facts!

Q: Why watch out for these boxes?

A: They answer the butterfly and moth questions you always wanted to ask.

zoom in on...

Bits and pieces
Look out for these boxes to take a closer look at butterfly and moth features.

Awesome facts
Watch out for these diamonds to learn more about truly weird and wonderful butterflies and moths.

Two pairs
of wings

Antenna

What are the differences between butterflies and moths? Most moths are nocturnal, which means they come out at night, while most butterflies fly during the day. Because of this, moths often have dark or dull wing patterns, while butterflies have brighter colours. Butterflies usually rest with their wings folded together, while moths spread their wings flat. Lastly, moths are hairier than butterflies.

OAK SILK MOTH

Forewing

Antennae

Proboscis (used
for feeding)

HELICONIUS BUTTERFLY

Moths and butterflies
have six legs, arranged
in three pairs.

Awesome facts

Lepidoptera have existed on Earth for over 70 million years. Today, there are more than 150,000 species (types) of butterflies and moths.

Hindwing

Abdomen
(body)

4

What are butterflies and moths?

Butterflies and moths are insects. Like all insects, they have six legs and two antennae (feelers). They belong to an insect family called *Lepidoptera* – Greek for 'scaly wing'. All *Lepidoptera* have four wings. Butterflies and moths are found all over the world, except in the icy polar regions.

Most moths only fly at night. The burnet moth (left) is unusual as it flies during the day. It lives on moors and meadows in Europe.

A red lacewing butterfly with its wings together (left) and spread out (below)

As these photos of a lacewing butterfly show, butterflies' wings are patterned on both sides. But many moths' wings only have patterns on the upper side.

Antennae

All moths and butterflies have two antennae on their heads. Butterfly antennae are 'clubbed' (thicker at the tips), while moths often have feathery antennae. Antennae are used for feeling and smelling things. Insects often use them to recognise each other when they meet.

zoom in on...

Scaly and furry

Butterflies and moths have tiny scales all over their wings. They're like a fish's scales, but much smaller. They give butterflies and moths their wing markings, which can help them to hide from their enemies or attract a mate. Besides scales on their wings, many moths have a kind of fur on their bodies, too.

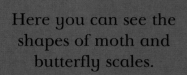

Here you can see the shapes of moth and butterfly scales.

Q: How do scales help moths and butterflies to stay safe?

A: Butterfly and moth scales rub off easily. This makes butterflies and moths slippery to touch, helping them to escape from dangers such as spiders' webs.

EUROPEAN CHALKHILL BLUE BUTTERFLY

On a butterfly or moth's wing, different-coloured scales are arranged in lines, shapes and dots to make up patterns. The tiny scales are too small for us to see normally, but we can see them under a microscope.

Close-up of a butterfly's wing

6

zoom in on...

Iridescent wings

MORPHO BUTTERFLY

Some butterflies have wings that seem to sparkle and change colour in the sunlight. They are called iridescent wings, and they are made up of special scales that contain many transparent layers. Light bounces around inside these layers, making the wings shimmer and shine.

Many moths have thick 'fur' on their bodies, and sometimes on their wings, too. This isn't the same as the fur on a cat or dog, or the hair on a human. Instead, it's made of the same material as scales, formed into a hair-like shape. Scientists think the 'fur' helps moths to keep warm, as they fly at night when it's cooler.

This *Automeris illustrus* moth flies at night and is very furry.

A single morpho butterfly can have more than 10,000 scales.

7

Most moths have tiny hooks on their forewings that fit into bristles on their hindwings. This links the two wings together, making them work like one big wing.

ATLAS MOTH

Wings and flying

All moths and butterflies have four wings altogether – two forewings and two hindwings. In butterflies, the forewings slightly overlap the hindwings. In moths, they are joined together. Moths and butterflies fly by flapping their wings in a figure-of-eight pattern.

PAINTED LADY BUTTERFLIES

The croesus moth has frilled wings.

The graphium butterfly has long wing 'tails'.

The common jay butterfly has wide wing tips.

While many butterflies and moths have simple oval or triangle-shaped wings, some have wings with frilly edges, extra-long wings or dangling wing 'tails'. These strange wing shapes may help butterflies and moths to recognise others of their own species.

GLASSWING BUTTERFLY

zoom in on...

Glasswings

Glasswings are butterflies that have wings that you can see through! Their wings are very light and delicate, with only a few scales to give them some markings around the edges. The rest of their wings are scale-free and transparent. This helps glasswings by making it hard for predators to see them in the rainforests where they live.

Earworm moths and hawk moths can fly at speeds of up to 32 km/h, faster than most other insects.

9

zoom in on...

Mating scents

Like many animals, moths and butterflies release scents called pheromones when they want to find a mate. The smell helps males and females of the same species to find each other. Many butterflies and moths have a very good sense of smell.

Male and female birdwing butterflies

Many moths use ears on the side of their body to sense the vibrations from a bat's squeak. The moth then tries to get out of the way before it gets eaten.

A female pale tussock moth gives off a scent to attract a male.

Awesome facts

Many butterflies can taste with their feet! They can tell if they've found the right plant to feed on, or lay their eggs on, the moment they land on it.

The hawk moth (right) feeds by night on the nectar found in honeysuckle. It uses its good sense of smell to track the plant down by its scent.

The male emperor moth (left) has huge fringes on his antennae. They increase the surface area of the antennae, making them extra-good at smelling. Some male emperor moths can smell a female up to 11 km away!

Super senses

Butterflies and moths have amazing senses, often far better than ours. Butterflies can see ultraviolet light, which is invisible to humans. They can see all around them, but the area in front and below them is magnified. This helps them to find particular types of flowers to feed on. Moths and some night-flying buterflies have ear-like hearing organs that can sense vibrations in the air.

zoom in on...

Scent pencils

In butterflies, it's only the male that releases scent when he wants a mate. A male has special hair-like organs called 'scent pencils' on his wings or abdomen. He uses them to shower scented dust onto a female, to make her feel like mating.

MALE OWL BUTTERFLY

In some butterfly species, the males have completely different colours and patterns from the females. Common eggfly butterflies from Australia are one example of this kind of butterfly.

MALE COMMON EGGFLY BUTTERFLY

Some scientists used to believe male and female moths found each other by sending radio signals with their antennae!

FEMALE COMMON EGGFLY BUTTERFLY

12

Finding a mate

Like most animals, butterflies and moths have
to mate in order to reproduce (have babies).
To mate, a male and a female of the same
species have to meet up. Male and female
moths usually find each other by their scent,
while butterflies often recognise each other
by their markings and flight patterns.

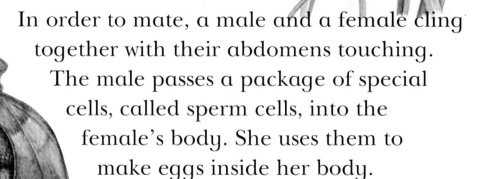

The courtship 'dance'
of the adonis blue

In order to mate, a male and a female cling
together with their abdomens touching.
The male passes a package of special
cells, called sperm cells, into the
female's body. She uses them to
make eggs inside her body.

Poplar hawk
moths mating

Q: How often do moths and butterflies mate?

A: Some species of butterflies and
moths live only a few days or weeks,
and mate only once or twice in
their lives. Others, especially the
males, can mate hundreds of times.

13

A monarch butterfly laying eggs

Q: How do female moths and butterflies know where to lay their eggs?

A: Moths mainly use their antennae to sniff out the food plants that will suit their babies best. Butterflies find their favourite plants by landing on lots of different plants and tasting them with their feet.

Eggs and babies

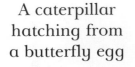

After mating, a female butterfly or moth is soon ready to lay her eggs. Some species drop their eggs as they fly along, and the caterpillars (babies) have to eat any food they can find. But most butterflies and moths lay their eggs on a particular food plant, so that when the eggs hatch, the caterpillars will have a supply of food waiting for them.

A caterpillar hatching from a butterfly egg

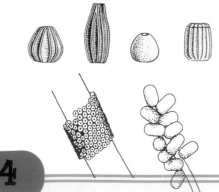

Eggs

Moth and butterfly eggs look like tiny balls, specks or grains of rice. Some species lay their eggs separately, while others lay them all together in a cluster.

zoom in on...

14

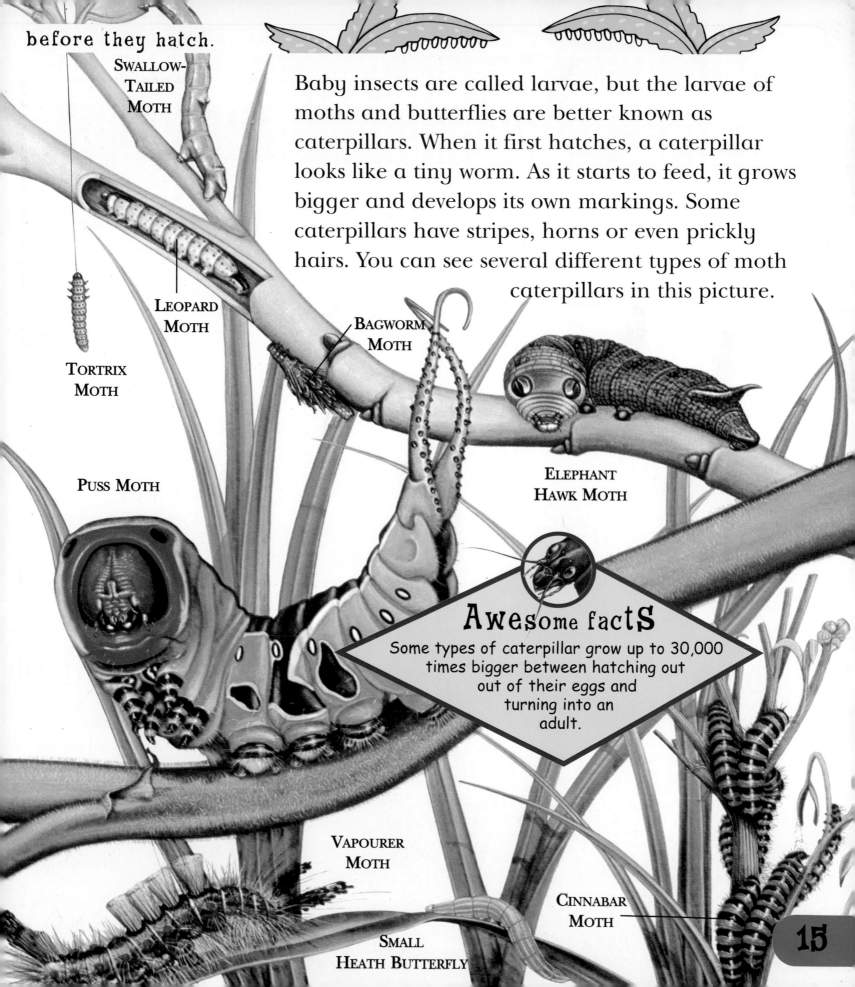

before they hatch.

SWALLOW-TAILED MOTH

LEOPARD MOTH

TORTRIX MOTH

PUSS MOTH

BAGWORM MOTH

ELEPHANT HAWK MOTH

Baby insects are called larvae, but the larvae of moths and butterflies are better known as caterpillars. When it first hatches, a caterpillar looks like a tiny worm. As it starts to feed, it grows bigger and develops its own markings. Some caterpillars have stripes, horns or even prickly hairs. You can see several different types of moth caterpillars in this picture.

Awesome facts
Some types of caterpillar grow up to 30,000 times bigger between hatching out out of their eggs and turning into an adult.

VAPOURER MOTH

CINNABAR MOTH

SMALL HEATH BUTTERFLY

15

Growing and changing

The word 'pupa' is Latin for doll, and some pupae look like little dolls.

Unlike human children, caterpillars don't look like small versions of their parents. Instead of just growing, they have to change completely to become adults. This changing is known as metamorphosis. Altogether, in its whole life cycle, a moth or butterfly goes through four different stages: egg, caterpillar, pupa and adult.

Swallowtail butterfly – caterpillar to adult

After hatching out of its egg, the swallowtail caterpillar eats almost solidly for 2-3 weeks. It grows and grows and then turns into a pupa. It attaches itself to a twig and grows a hard shell. Some caterpillars spin a silk cocoon around themselves instead.

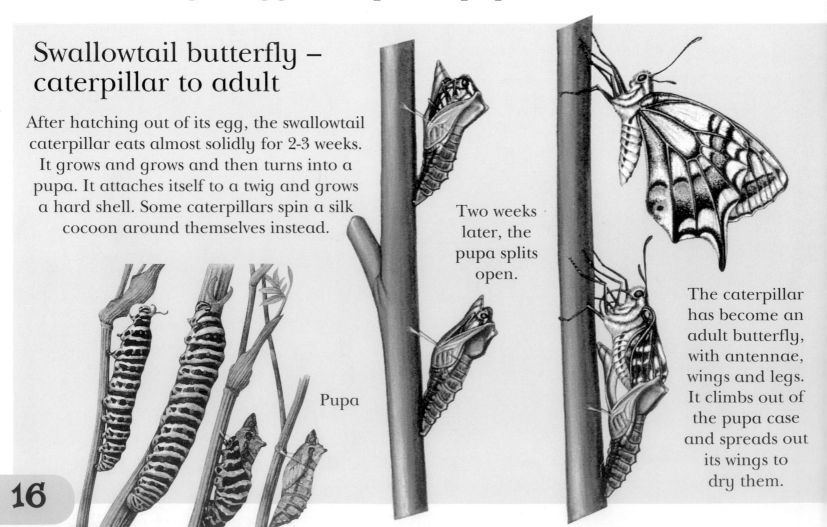

Two weeks later, the pupa splits open.

Pupa

The caterpillar has become an adult butterfly, with antennae, wings and legs. It climbs out of the pupa case and spreads out its wings to dry them.

Inside the pupa

When a caterpillar becomes a pupa, it doesn't just grow new body parts. Instead, its body breaks down completely into gooey slime. Its cells rearrange themselves, and the new butterfly or moth is built from scratch.

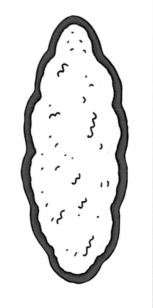

A sphinx moth pupa buries itself underground, in order to protect itself from predators while the caterpillar inside it is changing into an adult.

ROBIN MOTH

ADULT SWALLOWTAIL BUTTERFLY

It takes about an hour for an adult moth or butterfly to emerge from the pupa. Here, you can see a robin moth emerging.

1 The pupa case splits open.

2 The new adult pulls itself out of the case. Its wings are damp and folded up.

3 The adult pumps blood into its wings to open them out.

4 Once the wings have dried, the adult can fly away.

17

Food and feeding

Adult moths and butterflies have mouths that work like straws, so they can only eat liquid food. They suck up flower nectar, tree sap, or juice from rotting fruit. Caterpillars have chewing mouths, and can chomp through the leaves of plants such as cabbage and milkweed. Some moth caterpillars feed on other natural substances, such as wool.

A butterfly feeding on nectar, a sweet juice found inside flowers

Proboscis

Some moths never eat at all as adults. They only eat during the caterpillar stage of their lives.

SPHINX MOTH

The caterpillars below are feeding on a plant leaf. If a moth or butterfly lays a lot of eggs on one plant, the caterpillars can sometimes gobble up the whole plant after they hatch out. They feed by chewing leaves with their munching jaws called mandibles.

zoom in on...

The proboscis

An adult butterfly or moth's feeding tube is called a proboscis. It is designed to reach into flowers, fruit or puddles to suck liquid out. When not in use, the proboscis can be curled up in a coil beneath the head. In some moths, like the sphinx moth, above, the proboscis is longer than the moth's whole body.

Many butterflies have a favourite food plant. One plant that is enjoyed by many butterflies is the buddleia (below). This plant is so popular it is sometimes called the 'butterfly bush'.

COMMA BUTTERFLY

PEACOCK BUTTERFLY

RED ADMIRAL BUTTERFLY

TORTOISESHELL BUTTERFLY

Staying safe

Birds, spiders, bats, lizards and many other animals all like to snap up moths, butterflies and caterpillars. But they have plenty of ways to hide, escape or defend themselves. Adult moths and butterflies can fly away from danger. Many caterpillars eat poisonous plants and store the poisons in their bodies, making them poisonous to predators. Others have stinging spines or hairs, or give off a bad smell.

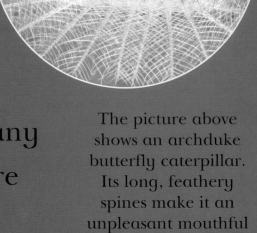

The picture above shows an archduke butterfly caterpillar. Its long, feathery spines make it an unpleasant mouthful for any passing predator.

Q: How does being poisonous help?

A: Poisonous moths, butterflies and caterpillars run the risk of being eaten, but the animal that eats them will feel very sick. This doesn't help the individual that is eaten, but it does put predators off eating the same insect again. So being poisonous helps the whole species to survive.

zoom in on...

LEAF MINER MOTH

Leafy hiding place

The caterpillar of the leaf miner moth lives inside a leaf. It burrows along between the two surfaces of the leaf, eating leaf cells and leaving a winding trail. When it becomes a pupa, the caterpillar wraps the whole leaf around itself as a protective case.

Poisonous insects often have bright stripes, spots or other markings to warn predators not to eat them. This is called warning coloration. Heliconid butterflies, burnet moths and zebra swallowtail caterpillars all have warning coloration. Some species that aren't poisonous copy, or mimic, the appearance of poisonous species so that they can stay safe, too.

This caterpillar's bright colours (above) warn predators that it could taste horrible.

Moths are often chased by bats, which use sound echoes to find their prey. A moth's fur helps to confuse bats by muffling these echoes. Some moths, like the death's head hawk moth, can also make noises to scare bats away.

BURNET MOTH

DEATH'S HEAD HAWK MOTH

Camouflage and disguise

Moths and butterflies are masters of camouflage and disguise. There are moths that look like bark, stone, wood or moss, and butterflies that look exactly like leaves. The tiger swallowtail caterpillar looks just like a bird dropping! Other species use disguise to look like something scary. The owl butterfly has spots that look like an owl's eyes, and some moths and butterflies imitate stinging insects.

Many moths and butterflies have dull, speckled patterns that help them to hide on tree trunks or rocks.

The scary snake in this picture is in fact not a snake at all, but a hawk moth caterpillar. When in danger, it can inflate part of its body to resemble a deadly viper, and wave it to and fro like a real snake.

peppered moths got darker too so they were still camouflaged.

The bee hawk moth looks like a bee.

This moth looks like a wasp.

This moth looks and walks like a fat, hairy spider.

Cunning copycats

Moths can't sting or bite, but some of them pretend they can by looking like other creepy crawlies. These three moths scare away their enemies by looking like a bee, a wasp and a scary biting spider. This kind of copying is called mimicry.

zoom in on...

There are six moths and butterflies hiding on these two pages. Can you find them all?

If a predator approaches, this io moth flashes its hindwings, revealing two large spots that look like a much bigger animal's eyes.

Leaf butterflies look just like leaves. They hide by sitting on plants among the real leaves. Some, like the kallima butterfly (right), are camouflaged only on the under-sides of their wings. When they fly away, their bright colours appear.

KALLIMA BUTTERFLY

Incredible journeys

Some butterflies and moths can fly huge distances. They travel, or migrate, to avoid cold winters or dry seasons, or to find food. The most famous migrator of all is the amazing monarch butterfly, but many other species migrate too, including the painted lady, red admiral and cabbage butterflies, and the sphinx moth.

Awesome facts

When monarch butterflies migrate, they always head for the same areas, even if they've never been there before!

Monarch butterflies live in North America. Not all monarchs migrate, just those born at the end of the summer. They fly up to an incredible 3,000 km south to Mexico and southern California, to spend the winter. Then they fly back again. They do this because the northern winter is too cold for them. The map on the right shows monarch migration routes.

NORTH AMERICA

California

Mexico

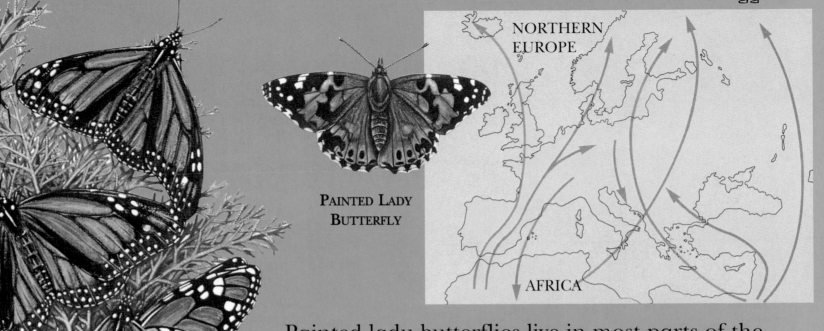

NORTHERN EUROPE

PAINTED LADY BUTTERFLY

AFRICA

Painted lady butterflies live in most parts of the world. Some groups of painted ladies migrate to spend the winter somewhere warmer than their usual home. European painted ladies, for example, fly hundreds of kilometres to parts of southern Europe or northern Africa for the winter (above).

When they arrive in Mexico, monarchs cluster together on conifer trees to rest.

During their migration flights, monarch and painted lady butterflies can fly up to 130 km per day.

zoom in on...

Moths and the Moon

Many moths use the Moon to help them find their way at night. By keeping the Moon on one side of them, they can make sure they are going in a straight line. Bright lights and flames confuse moths, because they mistake them for the Moon. If a moth sees a bright light and tries to stay on one side of it, it ends up flying around it and crashing!

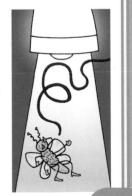

zoom in on...

Crop pests

Caterpillars have to eat a lot of food to grow enough to turn into adults. Unfortunately for us, they often hatch out on the food we grow for ourselves, and start devouring it. Many moth and butterfly species specialise in feeding on particular crop plants, such as cabbages and corn.

Cabbage white caterpillars eat cabbage leaves.

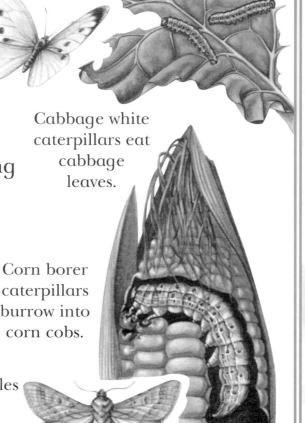

Corn borer caterpillars burrow into corn cobs.

Codlin moth caterpillars eat apples and other fruit.

Causing problems

Moths and butterflies are beautiful, but they can cause big problems for humans – especially farmers. The adults are usually harmless, but the caterpillars of some species eat their way through all kinds of crops, including grain, fruits and cotton plants. Other types of caterpillars can cause problems inside houses, by nibbling at clothes, books or carpets.

Q: Do moths really eat clothes?

A: Yes! The caterpillars of small moths called clothes moths really do nibble through clothes. In fact, they will eat anything made of fabric, including duvets, curtains, sheets and blankets, as long as they're made from a natural material such as cotton, silk or wool. They can eat big holes in clothes that are stored away in cupboards or wardrobes. Mothballs are balls of smelly chemicals that kill clothes moths. People put them in their cupboards to keep moths out.

Most clothes moths and crop pest moths are quite small but can be devastating.

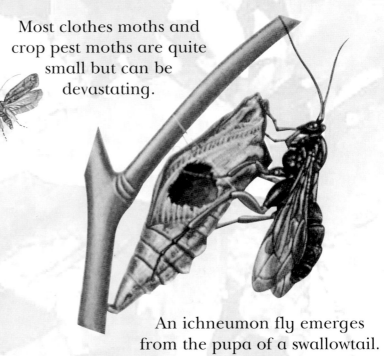

An ichneumon fly emerges from the pupa of a swallowtail.

Just as some moths and butterflies cause problems for humans, some other insects cause problems for moths and butterflies. For example, some ichneumon flies lay their eggs under a butterfly caterpillar's skin. When it hatches, the fly larva feeds on the caterpillar's body and takes it over. Finally, an ichneumon, not a butterfly, emerges from the pupa.

Moth and butterfly crop pests cost farmers millions of pounds worth of damage every year.

Helpful butterflies and moths

Many types of butterflies and moths can be very useful, both to humans and to other animals. They provide food for many other animal species – in fact, some animals, including some types of bats, only eat moths and nothing else. Butterflies and moths help plants make seeds by carrying pollen from one flower to another. Humans also use one type of moth, the silk moth, as the basis of a huge industry making silk thread and fabric.

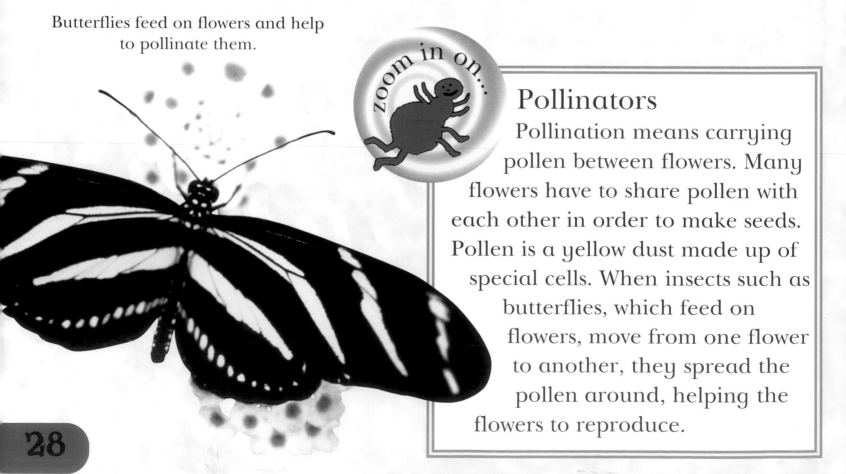

Butterflies feed on flowers and help to pollinate them.

zoom in on...

Pollinators

Pollination means carrying pollen between flowers. Many flowers have to share pollen with each other in order to make seeds. Pollen is a yellow dust made up of special cells. When insects such as butterflies, which feed on flowers, move from one flower to another, they spread the pollen around, helping the flowers to reproduce.

28

Q: Do humans really make money from moths?

A: Yes. Many silk farmers, traders and shopkeepers make their living from the silk moth, a large moth originally from China. On silk farms, silk moth caterpillars, also called silkworms, are fed their favourite food, mulberry leaves, until they are ready to pupate. The caterpillars spin silk around themselves to make protective cocoons. To harvest the silk, the farmers kill the pupae and unwind the long strands of silk from them. The strands are then twisted into threads, which can be woven into soft, shiny silk fabric. Silk is also used in other products such as shampoo and soap.

SILK MOTH

A model at a fashion show wearing a silk suit.

Beautiful butterflies and moths inspire designers to use their shapes and colours in jewellery designs.

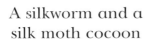

A silkworm and a silk moth cocoon

BIRDWING BUTTERFLY

Record holders

Few insects grow very big, but because of their large wings, moths and butterflies are among the biggest. The world's largest butterfly, the Queen Alexandra birdwing, has a massive wingspan of up to 31 cm. It's as wide as a dinner plate! The biggest moth is the atlas moth, which has a wingspan of 30 cm.

Many birdwing butterflies are very large. These are male and female Rajah Brooke's birdwings, which measure 18 cm across.

The monarch butterfly is the world's longest-lived butterfly.

An atlas moth – the biggest moth in the world.

The smallest butterfly is the western pygmy blue. It's only 1.5 cm across.

Awesome facts

Monarchs, the longest-lived butterflies, can survive for up to nine months. At the other extreme, some copper and blue butterflies live for just a few days as adults.

Glossary

Abdomen
One of the three body parts of an insect. All insects have three body parts – a head, a thorax and an abdomen.

Antennae
Feelers found on an insect's head. All insects have two antennae.

Camouflage
The way an animal blends in with its surroundings to escape being noticed by another animal.

Courtship
The way that a male and a female animal prepare for mating. They are often trying to impress each other.

Larva
A young insect. Larvae can look like a small version of the adult, or they can look completely different.

Lepidoptera
The group of insects to which butterflies and moths belong. It is a Greek word meaning 'scaly-wings'.

Mandibles
Mouth organs (jaws) used by insects to seize and bite prey.

Metamorphosis
The striking change some insects go through from larva to adult.

Migration
The long journey undertaken by some animals each year.

Nocturnal
Insects that rest during the day and are awake at night are nocturnal.

Pheromones
A smell given off by moths and butterflies to attract a mate.

Pollination
The process by which insects transfer pollen from one flower to another. In doing so, the plant is pollinated and can produce seeds.

Predator
A flesh-eater – an animal that hunts other animals for food.

Prey
An animal that is caught and then eaten by another animal.

Proboscis
The long, straw-like tube through which moths and butterflies feed.

Pupa
The stage through which butterflies and moths go between being a larva and an adult.

Species
The scientific word for a type of living thing. Animals of the same species can breed together.

Thorax
One of the three body parts of an insect. *See abdomen.*

Ultraviolet light
A type of light that humans cannot see. However, butterflies and moths can see ultraviolet light.

31

Index